# Around the Corner

**National Library of Canadian Cataloguing in Publication Data**

Main entry under title:

Around the corner
(Gage Cornerstones) For use between grades 1 and 2.
ISBN 0-7715-1404-2

1. Readers (Primary) I. Farr, Carolyn
PE1119.A75 2001      428.6      C2001-900880-5

**Illustrations/Photo Credits**
**6-7** Marion Stuck; **8-15** Michael Martchenko; **16-21** Bernadette Lau; **22-23** Photo Researchers Inc.; **24-29** Michael Martchenko; **31-32** Sunyoung Kim

**Editorial Team**
Joe Banel
Darleen Rotozinski
C. Samantha Vrakking

**Gage Production**
Bev Crann
Anna Kress

**Design/Art Direction
& Electronic Assembly**
Pronk&Associates

We acknowledge the financial support of the Government of Canada through the Book Publishing Industry Development Program for our publishing activities.

ISBN 0-7715-**1404**-2
1 2 3 4 5 GG 05 04 03 02 01
Written, printed, and bound in Canada.

# Around the Corner

Carolyn Farr        Jane Hutchison

Carol McGrail        Carol Pawlowski

**gage** EDUCATIONAL PUBLISHING COMPANY
A DIVISION OF CANADA PUBLISHING CORPORATION
Vancouver·Calgary·Toronto·London·Halifax

# Table of Contents

# Turn the Page

Poem by Carol McGrail and Jane Hutchison    Pictures by Marion Stuck

There's wonder in every book you read,
In every story and poem.
Turn the page and enter in
To adventures still unknown.

Within the pages of this book,
You'll take a trip with friends,
And see the many wonders
That Mother Nature sends.

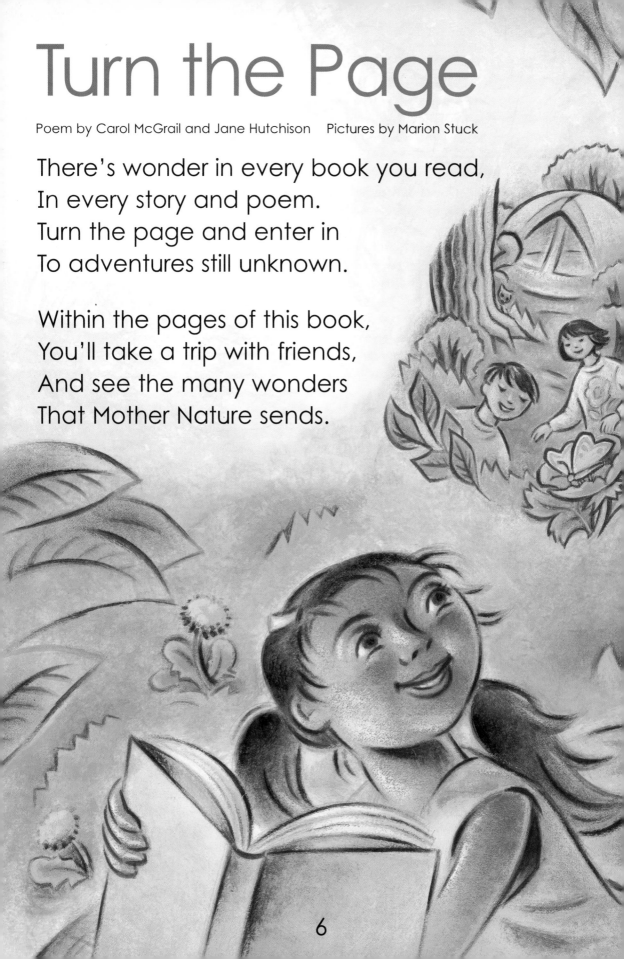

How about selling lemonade,
On a hot, hot sunny day.
Or laughing at knock-knock jokes,
To pass the time away.

Friends are waiting just for you
With stories to be told.
So turn the pages, one by one,
For adventures to unfold.

# The Sock Monster

Story by Carolyn Farr

Pictures by Michael Martchenko

"Where is it?" grumbled Bud. "Where is my sock? I'm going to be late for school."

Bud looked under his bed but he couldn't see
a thing.

"I'll get my flashlight," he thought.

Bud pointed his flashlight under his bed.

"Oh great!" he said. "There's my ball and my lost
library book. But where is my sock?"

Into the toybox he went. Toys and clothes flew
everywhere, but there was no sock.

Bud looked in his clothes hamper. He could not find his missing sock.

Suddenly he stopped. "Oh no," he thought. "It must be the sock monster.

Mom says the sock monster lives in the washing machine and eats our socks!"

"Mom! Come quick!" called Bud. "I think the sock monster ate my sock!"

"I've looked everywhere.

I've looked in my drawer and in my closet.

I've looked in my hamper and in my toybox.

I've looked under my bed, but my sock is not there.

The sock monster ate my sock!"

Just then, Bud looked down at his foot.

His foot looked very big.

"My foot feels funny," he said.

Bud pulled off his sock very slowly.

"Oops!" he giggled. "Here's my missing sock!"

Bud laughed and laughed.

"I'm the sock monster!"

# Night Lights

Story by Carol Pawlowski    Pictures by Bernadette Lau

"Are you ready to go?" asked Dad.

Mark and his sister Darleen got into the car. They had been planning this camping trip all week. They were going to go fishing and hiking. They were going to sleep overnight in a tent.

When they got to the spot by the big lake, they set up their tent.

Then they went hiking and saw lots of birds and animals.

The children went fishing and caught three rainbow trout.

Mark and Darleen helped their father make
a campfire.

After dinner they sang songs.

They all took turns telling scary stories.

What a time they had!

"It's getting dark," said Dad. "Time for bed."

They put out the fire with lots of water and sand.
There was not one sign of smoke.

Mark and Darleen wiggled into their sleeping bags.
They couldn't keep still. They tried and tried to
sleep but they heard so many scary sounds.

All of a sudden Mark yelled, "I want my night
light!"

"Just look outside," said Dad. "You have lots of night lights out there."

The children peeked outside the tent. They looked up into the night sky.

"Look at all the bright colours," said Darleen.

"Wow!  Awesome! Cool!" they whispered.

The children watched the lights dance across the sky.

"They are the northern lights," said Dad.

"You also have a full moon and the stars for night lights. Now you can go to sleep," he said.

Before long there wasn't a sound in the tent. Dad looked at the children. They were sound asleep.

Dad sat very still. He looked up into the sky and smiled.

Mother Nature had given the children a night light and now she put on a fireworks show for him.

# Northern Lights

The northern lights are an amazing show of colour.
They can be seen in the northern skies.
They are sometimes called the **aurora borealis**
[ah-**ROR**-uh BOR-ee-**AL**-is].

Red, blue, purple, and greenish-white are the colours of these marvellous lights.

The northern lights make many shapes. You can see arches, twists, swirls, and showers that dance across the night sky.

Aurora shapes can be hundreds of kilometres high and go for thousands of kilometres across the sky.

# The Lemonade Stand

Story by Carol Pawlowski    Pictures by Michael Martchenko

Ted grumbled to his friend, Kim, "It's so hot. It's too hot to do anything!"

"Yes, it's hot enough to fry an egg on the street," laughed Grandma, who was busy working in her garden. "When I was a little girl, we used to make lemonade and sell it at a lemonade stand. We sold lots of lemonade."

"Let's make a stand and sell lemonade!" said Ted.

Before long Kim and Ted had made a wonderful lemonade stand. They had lots of cool lemonade to sell.

They sat and sat.

They waited for the customers to come.

"Why don't we have any customers?" wondered Kim.

Along came a lady. "Would you like to buy some lemonade?" Ted asked.

"Oh, are you selling lemonade?" she asked. "You need a sign so that people know what you are selling."

The lady bought a glass of lemonade. She sipped it slowly and said, "Mmm! That's good!"

Ted got a board. Kim got some red and yellow paint. They made a big sign.

This is what it looked like:

Lminad 4 Sal

"Now we should get lots of customers," Ted said.

They sat and sat but no customers came. Soon Robin came along.

"What are you selling?" she asked.

"Read our sign," they said.

Robin looked at the sign and she giggled.

"No wonder you don't have any customers!"

Lminad 4 Sal

She helped them make a new sign.

Soon they had a long line of customers.

"Oh no!" cried Kim. "We're out of lemonade."

She hurried over to Grandma.

"Grandma, what are we going to do?" asked Kim.
"We don't have enough lemonade for all the
customers in the line."

Grandma smiled and called, "Come and get it! Free cold drinks!"

Everyone hurried to get a free cold drink.

Robin made a new sign.

"Here's your sign, Grandma!"

Everyone laughed!

# Lemonade Knock-Knocks

By Jane Hutchison    Pictures by Sunyoung Kim

Knock! Knock!

Who's there?

Anita.

Anita who?

Anita glass of lemonade.

Knock! Knock!

Who's there?

Harry.

Harry who?

Harry up and make me some lemonade, I'm thirsty!

Knock! Knock!

Who's there?

Wanda.

Wanda who?

Wanda glass of lemonade?

Knock! Knock!

Who's there?

Sue.

Sue who?

Sue sorry, it's all gone.

Knock! Knock!

Who's there?

Darryl.

Darryl who?

Darryl be lots of lemonade tomorrow.